The Tale of My Tail

Sarah Rae Gilbert

Published by Redwood Publishing, LLC
www.RedwoodDigitalPublishing.com

For more information, contact:
Sarah Rae Gilbert
www.daisytherottie.com
contact@daisytherottie.com

ISBN Paperback: 978-0-9975242-4-6
ISBN Hardcover: 978-0-9981760-0-0
ISBN eBook: 978-0-9975242-5-3

Library of Congress Control Number: 2016955621

Cover Design and Illustrations by Nancy Batra
Interior Design by Ghislain Viau

This book is dedicated to my extraordinary family.
For their immeasurable support and unconditional love, I am forever grateful!

My name is Daisy and I have just learned,

About something different and I am concerned.

It has come to my attention that some of my kind,

Do not have a tail on their behind.

But what if they're happy? What if they're glad?

What do they do without a tail to wag?

Or, what if it's me? What if I'm strange?

What if they tell me I need to change?

Say it's not true, please say it's not so!

I love my tail and I won't let it go!

They cannot make me – no how, no way!
And if they try, here's what I'll say,

I'm not changing a thing, no I am not!
I'm keeping my tail in this exact spot!

I'm not ashamed, I wear it with pride!
A tail is way too special to hide.

I'll be an example, I'll let everyone know,
That I believe all tails should grow!

If it's curly or furry, don't worry, that's fine!
You don't need to have one just like mine.

There's something about you, something unique,
And whatever that is, it's yours to keep!

Be proud of yourself and all that you do.
You were born to be special, born to be you.

So wag your tail with all your might!
Stay true to yourself, you'll be all right!

Let's show them we're happy, show them we're glad.
Let's show the world we have tails to wag!

Contact Daisy:

www.DaisyTheRottie.com

 www.instagram.com/imdaisytherottie

 www.facebook.com/ImDaisytheRottie